RICHARD |

HOW TOGO FOUND STRENGTH

CONTENTS

INTRODUCTION

This novel is about the life of a young boy called Togo. Even though he faced many difficult situations in his life, to the point of despair, he used those bad experiences to turn around that life as he rose to the pinnacle of success.

Togo became an orphan at the age of ten, and at twelve he was sent to work on the plantation in the rural part of Jamaica. After working on the plantation for a number of years, he ran away to Kingston, and got a job working in an old shipyard. One night he decided to stow away on a ship to America, where heo became a member of one of the most notorious Jamaican gangs in New York. He was arrested by the FBI, charged with money-laundering, and was sent to prison. Released from prison on parole and sent back to Jamaica, Togo then travelled to England, where he decided to share his story with other young people and encourage them not to make the same mistakes.

Togo is now the leader of a newly founded youth organisation known as Street Talk, where he uses his past experiences to turn around the lives of over 250,000 young people.

A POEM BY RICHARD BROWN

When will the leader stop and take a break,
When will they realise that they are making mistakes,
When will people get to understand that their lives are in a serious revolution?
We don't need a glass to see why people are living in poverty,
We don't need anyone to come and tell us how the system treats us as dangerous.

It is a worldwide recession upon all generations.
Worldwide recession.
They can't find any solution,
Worldwide recession.
Brother, what is your opinion?
Worldwide recession.
Stand still, all politicians.

If you read it in the Bible,
It is the book of prophecy.
When God took an oath, and that's no joke,
He said "Not one of my words shall pass away."
You better hear what I say, or else heaven and earth shall come to an end.
Let me tell you again,
When you are watching the TV
So much crime and robbery,
When you listen to the news
So much child abuse.
But all these things are the beginning of sorrow
It's like no hope for a better tomorrow
It is a worldwide recession.
They can't find any solution.

CHAPTER I
BORN TO A COLD WORLD

Deep in the parish of St. James, in a small rural district called Ammety, where cattle rearing was common in and around the village, near the pasture Sammy the large grey donkey had just woken up, stamping around furiously to make his first morning bray, while over at Mr Morris's farm, Cha-Cha the large golden rooster jumped off the roost, flapping his extremely large golden wings then bellowing his crow three times or more. In the fresh and cool morning breeze, far away you could hear the sweet singing of the nightingale and smell the sweet scent of the hibiscus flowers as they popped their roses open.

It was a very bright and lovely spring morning when Leeta gave birth to her fourth child. He was a very strong and sturdy-looking baby boy, of a very dark and rich complexion with plenty of black hair, and the face of an African maroon. His mother called him Togo. Two weeks later Togo was taken to the great riverhead to be blessed. In the eighteenth century the great river was known as the great magic river, with many tales and mysteries told about it. At the beginning of each leap year, seven other rivers would burst out of the head of the great river. The current of the water was so strong it would sweep through the valley and attempt to destroy the villages. The water was said to possess great healing power. It was so pure and clean that people would travel from miles away to bathe in it, or to fetch some to drink. On a clear and bright night when the moon was full, a monster would arise from the bottom of the river. It had seven heads with seven bright eyes, long hair and a silver tail like a mermaid's. The people of the village called it Bimbo the weeping monster. If Bimbo cried six times it

meant that six pregnant women would give birth to six important babies that night. But if Bimbo wept seven times it simply meant that somewhere around the world, seven heads of state would die the same night.

As a point of contact Leeta would grab Togo's arm as she repeated a prayer, then dip him in the water seven times to receive strength. "Togo is a special child. Yes! He's a light to the world and blessing in the eyes of men." Then his mother Leeta would light seven candles and place them on the bank of the river to burn until morning. Now you can understand why Togo is a blessing in disguise.

When Togo was five years old, his mother and father were separated by various circumstances. Leeta was left with four children living in a small wooden house built many years ago, before a great storm. It was very old-fashioned, with a tiny wooden window at the back, and at the front an eccentric, horseshoe-shaped wooden door.

Every morning at about 5.30am, Leeta would wake up listening for the sound of the 'Blue Dandy' bus. Then she would get dressed in her long red-and-blue skirt and her pink-and-white blouse, on her feet her one and only pair of black sandals which had been bought in the Christmas sales some years ago, and hurry to the main road so as not to miss the bus. If she did, she would have to walk about five miles to get to Cambridge, where she worked as a domestic helper.

Punchinella was the eldest of the four siblings. Her job was to be the caretaker until Leeta returned from work. Gal-Gal was the second, then Moonhead and Togo, and they had to fend for themselves until Leeta returned from Cambridge. Life could be very difficult.

Cambridge was a small town situated on the south side of St James. It was said to be the first town in Jamaica where African slaves were bought and sold. At this time Cambridge was thriving, with many small businesses such as supermarkets, bakeries and fine restaurants. It even had a large outdoor market just at the end of the main road.

Because Cambridge was the main centre of small business, every Saturday morning the small town would come alive, buzzing with people who would travel from east, west, north and south of Jamaica, as well as from nearby parishes such as Hannover, St Elizabeth and St Ann's Bay.

People were buying and selling many different kinds of goods, and everyone was determined to cash in on their last-minute shopping for Sunday. Cambridge has a very long history of colonisation – it was also where many middle-class families lived, the descendants of the many European, English among them, slave masters who lived there. These people were tall, very light in complexion, with long curly hair and bright blue eyes. They all looked alike.

CHAPTER 2
MY FATHER AND I

Every Saturday morning at approximately six o'clock Mr Armstrong, Togo's father, would wake up to a cup of Blue Mountain coffee, two fried dumplings, and a large jackfish that he caught the day before in the river just below his farm. After his meal, Mr Armstrong would get ready for his day's activity. Having served ten years or more in the Jamaica Defence Force (JDF), he was now a qualified retired Sergeant Major, and the captain and commander of the Cambridge Cadet Regiment. He would have a bath in the river, get cleaned and shaved, then put on his green khaki suit with red stripes down the sides of his pants. On his head he would wear a black police hat, looking like a brigadier general with a silver cane in his right hand, and on his feet he would wear size twelve shoes.

Mr Armstrong would then jump on his Ladies Wheel bicycle and ride it to nearby Ammety [speling?] to get his son Togo. Knowing that he was on his way, Leeta would get Togo to dress in his blue khaki suit along with his blue cadet hat, looking like a smart soldier boy. Leeta was very proud of her son, and very happy to see Mr Armstrong. As he entered the village, turning the corner by Dog Kennel Hill, Mr Armstrong would start blowing his silver whistle. At first it would sound like the whistle of old Tom the milkman, who rode around the village on his donkey every Saturday morning delivering milk to the neighbourhood, but it was not him, it was Mr Armstrong's whistle. As he blew along, hearing the whistle Gal-Gal and Moonhead would jump out of bed, rushing down Dog Kennel Hill at the speed of lightning to greet him.

He would then untie a large green box from the back of the bicycle and hand it over to Moonhead, while Gal-Gal sat on the crossbar, which was fun to see. When Moonhead entered the house with the box, Leeta and the other children would stand around waiting for it to be opened. Punchinella would pop the box open and suddenly there appeared many different kinds of fruit, such as mango, pineapple, oranges and some large, ripe golden bananas. At the bottom of the box there were some yams, corn on the cob and sweet potatoes, and wrapped in silver foil was a large jackfish which

Mr Armstrong had caught in the river the day before. Then Togo began to shout, "Mama, Mama, the eyes of the fish are very large and look scary, too scary for me!" Leeta replied, "Boy, that part of the fish is the sweetest part, and to buy this fish in the market would cost me a whole month's wages!" and then they all laughed out loud together.

After an hour or so it was time for Mr Armstrong to return to Cambridge, along with Togo and Moonhead, who were also members of the Cambridge Cadet Regiment. As they approached the square they could hear the mighty sound of drums beating – this was Mr Blackwell, the second in command at the Cambridge Cadet Regiment. More than three hundred and fifty boys were getting ready to fall in for parade, all dressed in their lime-green uniforms with blue-and-red stripes down the sides of their pants. Standing at their right side was a Browney, which is a tall wooden rifle made from mahogany wood. Then Mr Armstrong would move to the front of the platoon, getting ready to give his first command. There was a great moment of silence as he pushed his chest forward and bent back his shoulders then shouted, "Soldiers, attention!" In a swift movement the boys would turn ninety degrees left, then lift their rifles and slam them to the ground. Like an earthquake, you could feel the impact on the ground from miles away. Then Mr Armstrong would begin to speak, saying: "Boys, today our training begins for the twenty-fifth anniversary of our independent cadet fiesta. I would like you all to give your best performance on that day." Mr Armstrong was a very strict and fierce commander; no soldier would ever dare to speak when he was in command. Again at the top of his voice, he shouted, "Soldiers, quick march!" and immediately the drums started rolling and the bugles began to blow: you could hear the sweet sounds of military music playing from afar. The people all lined the street, dancing as the boys marched towards the cathedral singing, "Hooray, hooray, we're jolly good soldier boys, hooray, hooray, we're soldiers fit for war."

As they marched from the cathedral back towards the square, the people would greet them singing and cheering. More than one hundred and ninety-nine different coloured balloons were released into the atmosphere, a very beautiful sight to see as the balloons kept floating, then cascaded around and around in the summer breeze. Hibiscus roses and forget-me-not flowers were all given to the boys as they sang and marched through the crowd. As the day drew to an end, Mr Armstrong would give his final command, then the boys saluted him along with the crowd as they ended the parade. Everyone was feeling happy as they went home; after all, they had had a very lovely day.

A few months later came the big day for Mr Armstrong and the Cambridge Cadet boys. It was the 6th of August, Independence Day, when the British government along with the queen granted Jamaica their independence in 1966. More than twelve thousand cadet units joined together for this occasion; also alongside them were more than six hundred units from the Jamaica Defence Force (JDF).

The huge national arena was filled to capacity from side to side. People from every race, creed and class were there for one reason only, the celebration of Independence

Day. Suddenly the excitement began. Arriving at the main gate were the dignitaries. As the motorcade pushed through the crowd the people responded with great excitement. The presence of heavy security could be seen all around; there was a huge number of police, soldiers and alongside them the Great Eradication squad. As the motorcade reached centre stage, emerging from the black armoured cars were the Prime Minister, his lovely wife, the Governor General, a few top army majors and a few recognisable faces, the leaders and defenders of the nation. The show was about to begin.

Now it was time for them to address the Nation. First on the platform was the Prime Minister, greeting the people, "Ladies and gentlemen, comrades and friends, I greet you in the name of peace and love. Today is a special day, to see everyone coming together standing as a great nation. Power is the only argument that satisfies man. We can only possess power if we unite as a nation."There was a moment of silence, and as he continued the crowd responded with great cheers and admiration.

Next to appear on the platform was the Governor General, looking sharply dressed in his black, green and yellow suit, a symbol of the national flag. As he began addressing the people, he said, "Brothers and sisters, boys and girls, I stand before you in the name of freedom and liberty. Today is a victorious day, to see our people standing together as one. This day would not be possible if our leaders of yesterday had not stood up strong and bold. I am speaking about great leaders like Marcus Garvey, Paul Bogle, Daddy Sam Sharp and a fearless black woman called Nanny, who was of the Maroon tribe. Alongside them were George William Gordon, Norman Washington Manley, Sir Alexander Buster Manatee and Miss Louise Bennett.

"These men and women were bold and fearless. They fought tirelessly for us to stand here today." Just as he was coming to the end of his speech, from

the east side of the national arena you could hear a very strong and loud voice. It was the sound of the great one, Sir Adolphus Phillip Armstrong.

Now it was time for thousands of cadet boys to demonstrate and perform some of their many military skills, one of which was the great march past. As they marched towards the front of the arena, dressed in all kinds of military colours, the drums began to roll and the bugles to blow. You could also hear the loud sounds of military cymbals as they crashed and echoed around the stadium.

Mr Bennett, the Chief Commander of the Jamaican Defence Force, was in charge of six hundred soldiers. They too were about to perform the twenty-one-gun salute. As they marched past the crowd, suddenly they hoisted their rifles onto their right shoulders pointing towards the blue skies, and immediately there was a roar of thunder as the bullets exploded in the air. The crowd cheered as you could see great flashes of fire before the smoke cascaded in the open air. Then for a moment there was a great silence as the national flag was raised, then the people stood and sang the national anthem whilst the band played.

Over the years music and art have played a great role in the great culture of Jamaica, and now it was time for the big performance. The Rastafarian movement was then getting very popular in Jamaica, and these men had sung and composed some of the most cultural and conscious music the world had ever known. Appearing on stage was the crown prince of reggae music Dennis Emmanuel Brown, singing one of his greatest hits "No Man is an Island". After that we saw many more performances from people like Peter Tosh and Jacob Miller from big bands like Third World, and also Black Uhuru. Then suddenly the stage was clear and the light went low, for now appearing was the musical legend, the greatest songwriter and performer the world had ever known, Sir Honourable Robert Nester Marley – more commonly known as Bob Marley. As he began to sing, greeting the people with "We're Jamming", he jumped from left to right whipping his dreadlocks, and they responded with great excitement. He continued to sing many more hits and then finally recalled the leaders onto the stage and requested that everyone join hands as he closed with "One Love". There was such unity on a tremendous day in the history of the people.

As the day continued the people went on to enjoy themselves with delight. It is said that peoples with a strong culture always represent that strength in their food, and over the years Jamaica has produced some of the most delicious and authentic dishes blended with many different herbs and spices. All around the stadium you could smell the essence of great Çaribbean food, which makes you feel hungry – ackee and saltfish, yes of course, the national dish of Jamaica, curried goat served with white rice and salad, steamed callaloo served with fried dumplings and the famous jerk chicken served with rice and peas, to name but a few. Then don't forget some of the richest natural juices you have ever tasted, such as carrot juice, sour sap juice, Irish moss and linseed, sorrel blended with fresh ginger, peanut punch and many more. Those juices have now been marketed all over the world, representing the culture of Jamaica.

There is an old proverb in Jamaica, "Me belly full, but me hungry," which means that there is so much natural food around the people are spoilt for choice, and yet they say that there isn't enough to eat. Anyway, donkey say the world ain't level, ha ha ha! I have to laugh; it's just a proverb. As time goes on, these days Jamaica has been going through many changes. The people are still fighting to liberate themselves from mental slavery, and also against gun- and knife-crime. As we know, only the people can emancipate themselves by freeing their own minds. There is a famous poet who says, "When will the leaders stop and take a break, for them to realise that they are making mistakes? When will the people get to understand that there life is in a serious revolution?"

However, the facts of life continue. Mr Armstrong was now getting old, and at 65 was no longer the commander in chief of the Cambridge Cadets Boys; Mr Blackwell had been appointed in his place. Instead he now ran a small woodcutting business on the outskirts of Cambridge, supplying the community with logs, timber and trees. His busiest period was towards the end of October, when people would come from all over to acquire their logs for Bonfire Night. All around the village you could see people lighting all kinds of different fires and hear the sounds of rockets as they echoed across the sky, while in the square the big Bonfire Night celebration began. All the children would come together around the fire chatting and laughing, telling Anansi stories as they sang their bonfire songs, songs like "How water walk go a pumpkin belly", "Donkey want water, hold him Joe" and many more. Mr Armstrong was a very wise and clever old man, very loving and known in and around the community.

Togo was now twelve years old, and still attended the Cambridge Cadet Youth Club. Usually after training he would pop by the sawmill to see his dad, to have a chat and banter. One day when he finished training he hurried down Pimento Lane towards the mill to see his dad, but surprisingly he was not there, so he continued on home to tell his mother.

It was late in the evening, and so it was time for dinner. Leeta was a very good cook; the people in the village called her Cookie. Every Saturday she would cook cowfoot soup along with sweetcorn. Already all the other children were sitting around the small wooden table, gazing hungrily at their mother, waiting to have their soup. Suddenly there was a loud bang at the little horseshoe door, and surprisingly it was Togo, looking very tired and thirsty, not even remembering to greet his other brothers and sisters as he rushed through the short passage towards the small kitchen saying, "Mama, Mama, Dad was not at the mill today." Leeta quickly turned around, looking at Togo with astonishment, and replied, "Boy, did your father give you any money for school tomorrow?" "No ma'am," Togo replied. "I did not see him by the mill today at all." In a hurry, Leeta served the children their dinner as she complained, "I have spoken to your father about that rum drinking, now it seems like the rum has got the better of him." Then she began to laugh: "You see ya now, chicken, merry hawk is near. Too much rum drinking, he drinks too much for an old man."

Every Friday night after leaving the mill, Mr Armstrong and his men would hurry down Primento Lane, where they would stop by the little Red Rooster pub. They would drink white rum and cow's milk until late Saturday morning. Yes, of course, after all their hard day's work, I suppose a man gets to enjoy his leisure while he's yet strong.

It was now Sunday morning, hot chocolate tea served with ackee and saltfish with boiled banana, then for dinner, spicy jerk chicken served with rice and peas and green salad, together with fresh-squeezed carrot juice; that was a typical Sunday menu, and for dessert Leeta would serve a slice of potato pudding. After dinner it was time to go to visit Mr Armstrong in Cambridge. It was raining very heavily, the weather was looking bad. As Leeta and the children hurried down the little footpath approaching the bridge, the water was rising slowly, the river lapping the tops of its banks. When they tried to cross over the bridge, the current was sweeping it from side to side, so they all held hands to make a human chain, locking tightly together, pulling each other across. Then they hurried down Horse Past Hill, where the Blue Dandy bus was arriving. They were all soaking wet when they got safely aboard.

About an hour or so later they arrived in Cambridge. It was late in the evening, and starting to look very dark; when they left the main road heading through the valley it was pitch black. There was no electricity running through the valley, so they were greeted with the sounds of the bush crickets and thousands of lights from the 'peeny wallies'. As they neared the house they could hear someone snoring very heavily. They pushed the door and went in and saw it was Mr Armstrong, well asleep sitting up in his little wooden rocking chair. He hadn't even remembered to remove his boots from his feet. Hurriedly Moonhead struck a match and lit the little oil lamp, while Leeta shouted, "Adolphus, Adolphus, wake up man! It's Sunday evening, what you doing sleeping?" Suddenly Mr Armstrong popped his eyes open, looking confused and afraid. Then Togo grabbed at his big strong arms, saying accusingly, "Dad, Dad are you drunk?" Mr Armstrong jumped up and burst out laughing. "No, my boy, I'm not drunk, just tired and decided to take a nap in my chair." Moonhead stood there staring at Mr Armstrong, and his thoughts just popped out. "Dad I know you very well, do you think it's funny?".

"Gal-Gal, set the table, Punchinella, get the plates, and boys, make yourselves useful," said Leeta, then suddenly turning around with authority in her voice, ordered Mr Armstrong, "Go make yourself presentable and come and have something to eat." After dinner they all had a long talk then went off to bed.

On Monday morning Leeta got up early and woke up Punchinella; being the eldest, it was her job to take the others back home and get them ready for school, while Leeta accompanied Mr Armstrong to see Mr Williams for his monthly appointment at the Cambridge General Hospital. Since Cambridge was a mostly middle-class town, it was said to be one of the best hospitals in the country, known for its medically advanced equipment and many specialist doctors and caring nurses. Leeta and her family had attended the hospital for many years, but this time Mr Armstrong had a problem.

After waiting for two hours or more finally they went in to see Mr Williams. "Good morning doctor," grunted Mr Armstrong.

"Good morning Adolphus," he replied. "I noticed that you missed your last month's appointment, so I was getting a bit worried about you." These men were no strangers to each other, and knew when to have a good laugh. Going back to his notes, the doctor said, "At your last visit you were complaining about a pain in your lower right side, and your blood tests results show some abnormalities. I am not here to frighten you, but as your doctor and friend it's not good news. I'm afraid you have a chronic illness, it's kidney disease."

Now that was the last thing Leeta wanted to hear. All at once a sad and lonely feeling came over her, as in her mind she began to think "Am I going to lose Mr Armstrong?", but worst of all, "What am I going to tell the children?"

Doctor Willie continued to speak. "Adolphus, there is no cure for this disease, but there is a way it can be controlled by dialysis while waiting for a kidney transplant. I hope when we meet at your next appointment, we will be able to come up with a plan that will suit your needs. So I wish you and your family the best of luck. Have a good day, and see you soon."

However, it seems the discovery of Mr Armstrong's illness was too late. A few weeks later, he was found dead at his home in Cambridge.

CHAPTER 3
EXPOSED TO THE WORLD AROUND YOU

Therefore as the months and years went by the Armstrong family adjusted to many changes. It is so true when people say one hand washes the other, or a chain is as strong as its weakest link. Now Leeta had to work seven days a week to maintain her family. Punchinella got a live-in job in the city and only on special holidays was she allowed to visit her family, while Gal-gal moved to Cambridge to live with Ms Hortense. Leeta has worked for the Hortense family for over fifteen years, so Gal-gal was no stranger to them. They were one of the longstanding middle-class families living in and around Cambridge, and, delighted with her progress in school, decided to put her forward for a scholarship attending Cambridge Comprehensive School. Moonhead, who was sixteen, was about to graduate from Woodmill Comprehensive High with a certificate in mechanical engineering, and Togo, now thirteen, was in second grade at the same school as his brother. He liked to play football, which he played very well, but his favourite pastime was to play marbles. It was now December, and the new marble season had begun. Every evening after school, Togo and Rommel would hurry down to Primento Lane to meet Bunbun and the other boys, then they would play marbles until late afternoon.

Leeta started worrying about Togo because of his low grades and his late returns from school, so she decided to contact Mr Hughes, the principal of Woodmill Comprehensive High, by sending him an urgent letter through the post.

Leeta wrote:

Dear Mr Hughes,
Good day to you sir, I hope you are fine and in the best of health.
You see sir, I have noticed that my boy Togo has been coming home
from school very late in the evenings, I was wondering if he was
having any extra lessons for his upcoming examination? Since
the death of his father two years ago the boy has changed a lot. I
understand that he is a teenager now and as such, as is the case
with most male teenagers would rather prefer to have their fathers
speaking to them than listen to their mothers.
Please sir, I am therefore asking you if you could have a word or
two with him away from your busy schedules.
Yours truly
Leeta Armstrong.

Mr Hughes received Leeta's letter and decided to run an investigation
into Togo's whereabouts in the afternoons. Monday was a very bright and
sunny afternoon, and the day at Woodmill had come to an end, so all
the children were heading towards the big main gates as they hurried to
get home from school. As usual Mr Hughes was gazing through his office
window, making sure that the school compound was cleared. Suddenly
there were Togo and Rommel hurrying across the street, heading down
towards Primento Lane. As Mr Hughes already felt suspicious about them,
he quickly jumped up from his chair, grabbing his leather jacket, and
hurried out of his office towards the gate. As the boys reached the end of
the lane, they were spotted by Mr Hughes heading towards the old hospital
yard, and at the gate there was Bun-bun waiting, along with a group of boys
from Corner Street, all getting ready to play their favourite game of marbles
called "winner takes it all".

At once the game began. As the boys pitched their marbles and danced
around the ring in came Bunbun, one of the greatest marble pitchers of all
time. As he began to pitch with tremendous force from the far end (bang
bang), 32 marbles scattered from the ring. The boys began to skip like
gladiators around the ring, then Bunbun shouted, "Nobody move, nobody
get hurt. All hands off the dirt, it's winner takes it all!"

Suddenly there was a tremendous shout from the hospital gate. It was

Mr Hughes. "Now I know what you boys are doing after school, Togo and Rommel. I want you both to report to my office in the morning." At once all the boys grabbed their marbles and dashed through the old hospital gate, and ran home across the stop light heading towards Mango Lane.

On Tuesday morning all the children were arriving for school 8 o'clock sharp for inspection. Mrs Dorothy Mitchell, the Vice Principal at Woodmill Comprehensive High, was very strict and straightforward, not willing to support any nonsense at all during her inspection. All pupils must be appropriately dressed in their school uniform, wearing black tie along with their black shoes, and all hair must be properly combed; those were her requirements.

As all the children began to arrive at the auditorium, standing at the front of the building was Mrs Mitchell. I guess Mr Hughes must have had a word with her yesterday about the boys playing marbles by the old hospital yard, because as Togo and Rommel headed towards the auditorium, Mrs Mitchell shouted, "Not so fast, you two boys. Mr Hughes would like to have a word or two with you after devotion." Togo and Rommel looked at each other in surprise, thinking about the consequences they would face when they entered Mr Hughes's office.

After an hour or so, the morning devotion ended and all the children went to their classes, but Togo and Rommel were standing before Mr Hughes in his office. He began to remind them about the policy at Woodmill Comprehensive High. "The policy in this school stands for quality and excellence, and I do not think for a moment that playing marbles in your uniform represents that! And so I have to remind you two that these unscrupulous actions carry very serious penalties. However, because the new school year has just begun, I will not suspend you two, but I will give you a daily task to carry out. Every evening after leaving school, you will write me 250 words telling me what you have accomplished in school that day, then you will present it to me in my office the next morning. This assignment will be carried out for two consecutive weeks. Now I hope that you will find time to enjoy your evenings after school. Got that? So have a good day, boys, and see you tomorrow morning."

Leeta noticed that there had been many changes in Togo's attitude. He would get home from school a bit earlier, and after having his dinner he then started to do his school work. Leeta was delighted to see the progress Togo was making, and had already congratulated Mr Hughes about it. Now she was very happy.

CHAPTER 4
THE DEATH OF LEETA

As usual, Leeta worked hard to support her family; she was even thinking about reopening Mr Armstrong's woodcutting business in Cambridge. However, she had recently started to feel unwell when she attended her monthly appointment at Cambridge General Hospital. She was suffering from high blood pressure, and Doctor Williams noticed that after prescribing weeks and weeks of medication, she still had not experienced any significant changes. He had started to feel concerned about Leeta, and decided to have a talk with her.

It was Monday, a very busy morning for Leeta; after sending off her children to school, she hurried down to Cambridge to meet with Doctor Williams. On her way to the hospital, she began to experience severe headaches and dizzy spells, and when she arrived at the main entrance, Mrs Carmen the receptionist recognised her and sent her immediately to see Doctor Williams. As usual, Leeta went in and greeted him, but when they started to discuss family matters, he said, "Now that you are a single parent, I've been wondering, how you are coping with your family? Looking at you, dear, I can see a lot of stress in your eyes, and unfortunately your BP measures 180/95. Surely you can see that it is now on the high side? I will have to prescribe higher doses of the medicines you are currently taking. However, I would like to remind you that the best way to control your BP is to cut down on your salt intake and do a bit more exercise. I also realise that this is a very hard thing to ask of you, but I would really like you to take one week off work and to do a bit of exercise when you are at home. I hope all will be well with you, and I will see you at the end of next month for your appointment. Goodbye and have a good day."

Immediately Leeta left the hospital, she began to think about what Doctor Williams had said to her. She was also thinking to herself how she would break the news to the children.

On Saturday evening, Leeta cooked her favourite meal for the weekend, Caribbean stewed peas made with red peas and small pieces of oxtail, served with Uncle Ben's long grain white rice. It was a very tasty, mouth-watering dish. After dinner, it was time for Ananci's story. Leeta told the story about how brother Ananci tricked brother Tokema so he could marry the princess. It was very funny and so they all had a good laugh before they went to bed.

About four in the morning, Leeta woke up experiencing a severe headache and a terrible pain in her left side. With a tremendous scream, she shouted, "Togo Togo, can you wake up Gal-Gal and tell her go to the kitchen and fetch me the garlic?"

It was raining very heavily that morning, and it was a bit cold and dark. There was no electricity running through the small kitchen, so Gal-Gal was unable to see well. However, she found the garlic – but it was too late. It seems Leeta had suffered a terrible stroke in the middle of the night. So when Gal-Gal finally arrived at her bedside, Leeta was dead. She never even got a chance to say goodbye to her children.

And so for the second time, Togo and his brother and sisters experienced tragedy in their family. After the deaths of Mr Armstrong and Leeta, things weren't looking too good for them at all. Punchinella, the eldest girl, still worked in the city while her sister Gal-Gal was now living full-time with Ms Hortense in Cambridge. Moonhead, now seventeen years old and a fine young man, worked and lived with his girlfriend Rebecca in Panini town, while Togo was sent to live on a farm with his uncle Collie in Westmoreland. Mr Armstrong seldom spoke about his brother Collie, and unfortunately Togo had never got the chance to meet him before, but at least he seemed delighted to go and live with him.

It was late Saturday afternoon when Togo arrived in Westmoreland, dressed in his green cadet uniform and green cadet hat, looking very smart as usual. Waiting by the bus station was his Uncle Collie along with his lovely wife Olive. Suddenly, as Togo emerged from the old Blue Dandy bus, he could hear his uncle's voice shouting, "Togo, Togo, come over here boy!" and immediately he turned around, there were his uncle and Olive. They too were very delighted to meet him. When Togo walked over to greet them, Uncle Collie grabbed him by the hand whilst his wife hugged and kissed him. Collie said, "How are you, son?" and Togo replied, "I am fine, sir."

Collie then said, "How are your brother and sisters doing?" Togo replied, "Sir, they are doing fine as well."

"I am delighted to see you," Collie went on. "I would like to say how much I and my wife feel about the passing of your mother Leeta; we are so very, very sorry. I suppose it has been now two long years since I hadn't got the chance to visit her. Ever since the death of my brother Armstrong, I have begun to feel a bit concerned about her family, but now she too has passed away. I know how you all feel about it. However, I must say how happy I felt when I heard you had chosen to come and live with us. As you can see, son, it is only me and my wife who live here. Tooksi, my eldest daughter, got married and migrated to her husband's country two years ago, while Michael, my youngest son, is working as a lawyer over in St Ann's Bay. I hope that you will be very happy living with us here."

"I like this house, sir," said Togo, "because it is very big, but I was thinking, where would I attend school?"

His uncle replied, "Don't worry son, my wife Olive has already taken care of that. Olive," Collie shouted, "Tomorrow morning, I would like you to accompany Togo to see Ms Campbell." She was the principal of Jacksville Comprehensive High. Collie was a very well-known farmer in the community, one of the lucky ones who owned one of the grandest farmhouses in the estate. Jacksville Comprehensive High, where Togo would attend school, was also part of the community estate.

Westmoreland has been known as the garden parish of Jamaica. It is very flat and fertile. Sugar cane is the main source of income. All around the parish, you could see large plantations of sugarcane stretching from east to west, with large rivers and streams running across the plain. Water played a very important role in the fast-growing sugar-cane industry. The parish of Westmoreland is a very historical place. In 1833, after the abolishment of slavery, Daddy Sam Sharp led one of the greatest rebellions at the tender age of 31, determined to make sure that all ex-slaves should have the right to own a plot of land. Collie's forebears were among those who finally became owners of land then, and from that time until now, the land has been handed from generation to generation. Collie now owned some of the largest sugar plantations in Westmoreland.

Togo woke up early each and every morning, at approximately 6 o'clock. After having his first meal of the day, he'd then rush down to the farmhouse to feed more than 250 red hens. Knowing that Westmoreland is a very fertile place, he would also make sure that the hens had enough water to last them through the day. The reaping season of the sugar cane had already begun, and so the farm was very busy. After feeding the hens, Togo would then deliver more than 20 kilos of meat, 4 bags of rice and 10 dozen eggs to the butler by the canteen, to feed the hardworking men who worked in the fields and operated the mill by the boiler house. The water irrigation system was very important in the production of sugar. Every morning before Togo left the farm, he would make sure that enough water was flowing through the system. If by chance the water system was closed, the mill would begin to overheat, then the production of sugar would grind to a stop.

One morning after Togo had delivered the food to the butler, he totally forgot about turning on the water for the cooling of the mill. Suddenly, there was a loud noise coming from the boiler house, as loud as the sound of an explosion. It was the mill beginning to overheat. Collie immediately went to check the water system, and there it was: the water was off. Now Togo found himself in a bit of trouble with his uncle. So Collie decided that when Togo returned from school, he would make sure that he received a fine tongue-lashing.

In the early afternoon, after Olive had served Collie's meal, it was time for him to indulge. Usually, he would sit down on the couch by the kitchen while smoking a very strong cigar. He was a very lovely old man; however, he was also not very easy to get along with. Usually Togo would come home from school then have a snack before he rushed straight down to the farmhouse tocollect the large amount of eggs the hens had laid throughout the day. Just as Togo was about to walk out the gate, Collie spotted him. "Togo, Togo!" he shouted. "Can you spare me a moment so I can have a word with you?" At once Togo began thinking to himself, "I wonder what this is all about?" then his uncle elaborated by saying, "Boy, today we ran into a very serious problem with the mill, caused by overheating. And so the production of sugar will have to stop for a while. Now I would like you to explain to me how and why did you forget to turn on the water system? Togo, I would like to remind you that Michael, my son, operated that system for over ten years, and never forgot to turn it on his whole life. So my son, I would like to assure you that if ever this happens again, I guess you would have to leave this farm."

CHAPTER 5
RUN AWAY TO KINGSTON

Togo was now fifteen, and already thinking about leaving his uncle soon. And so after all his uncle had said and all the hard work on the farm, he decided that enough is enough, and ran away to Kingston one morning. After all those years, Togo had never got the chance to visit his sister Punchinella, who worked in the city. He knew that Kingston was a very large city and could be dangerous, especially at night, yet to him it was a risk worth taking as he set out, saying to himself "A man has to do what man has to do."

On Monday morning, having arrived in Kingston the night before, and slept rough, Togo decided to walk by to have a look at the old shipyard. As he approached the big Iron Gate, sitting in the security shed was a man dressed in a grey suit, looking very handsome and quite smart; this was Mr Robinson, the owner and manager of the yard. Although the yard was out of operation, it was still busy. People still went in and out, and many were doing documentaries of the old ships, especially that of Henry Morgan, one of the first pirates of the Caribbean, so it was not unusual for Togo to have a look around.

By 6pm, the shipyard was about to close. All the visitors headed towards the huge Iron Gate for home, and Togo was no different. He had been thinking about finding a place in the yard to sleep, but it was not possible because there was a night security guard. Just outside the gate, by the side of the road, there was a fleet of abandoned cars. Maybe they had been seized and left there by the police, or they were there for no apparent reason, but

Togo was delighted when he saw them, because he knew at least he had found a place to sleep for the night.

It was now 9pm and getting a bit dark. The security guard had not yet arrived on duty, so Mr Robinson seldom passed by to have a quick stroll around the yard. Just by the side gate a used station wagon car was parked, looking fairly in good condition, and as Mr Robinson approached it he could hear someone snoring heavily. As he drew nearer he decided to have a look, and there was Togo, well asleep in the back of the car. At first Mr Robinson was going to call the police, then he thought for a moment, saying to himself, "Is this person out of his mind!"

Suddenly, Togo arose from his sleep, looking very frightened and confused. When he realised that someone was watching him through the window of his car, he quickly opened the door and stepped outside. Mr Robinson was looking at him with amazement and disgust as he shouted at him, "Boy, who are you and where are you from?"

Togo thought for a moment, then replied, "My name is Togo, sir, and I came from the country and have nowhere to live."

For a second time, Mr Robinson shouted at him. "My friend, do you realise how dangerous it is around here? The police are now on patrol, and if by chance they catch you sleeping in this old car, first you get two years in jail for street loitering, then you also spend six months on hard labour in the general penitentiary, and that I could not wish for any young man."

Mr Robinson was a very kind-hearted man, and was already thinking about helping Togo. As he gazed across at the security box, where the night watchman was not yet on duty, he told Togo to spend the night working as a security guard. Then he continued, "I will come to see you in the morning."

Being a well-trained cadet and the son of Mr Armstrong, an army officer and cadet commander, Togo was no stranger to such tasks. The morning after, Togo was already up getting ready to go out on duty. It was a beautiful morning and the sky was bright, the old shipyard already getting busy with visitors, when in came Mr Robinson. As he drove through the main gate, there was Togo sitting in the security box, looking very relaxed. Mr Robinson reached over and threw him a brand new security uniform. Then Togo walked towards the main gate, looking very sharp as usual, and with a huge smile on his face. Mr. Robinson was very happy for him, so he walked with him around the yard, telling him what he expected from him. After a while, he then showed him a reasonable-sized bungalow which contained everything a young man would ever want, and handed over the key to him. "This is where you will stay."

All at once Togo began to see a turnaround in his life, and to feel very happy. Having a job and a place to live, he was now an independent man. Kingston is a very vibrant place, with lots of entertainment, an ideal place for a young man to gain experience for his early life. It was a very challenging way of life for Togo, but at least he began to feel a sense of responsibility – and every Friday and Saturday night, after work, Togo would get smartly dressed and head down for entertainment at the Pegasus night club. After a few months, Togo was one of the most popular guys around.

One night when he entered the club, he was invited by one of his best friends, Pinky-Loo, to have a drink by the bar. Togo now had a secret admirer, and her name is Nancy Morgan the bartender. Nancy was a very fine-looking girl with a dark, rich complexion and a sense of beauty in her eyes. She was also known to be a very good belly dancer. As the night went on, Togo invited her to have a dance on the floor, and there they were: it was love at first sight.

A few weeks later, when Togo and Nancy had got to know each other better, he was invited by Nancy to meet her father, Derek Morgan, at his Red Hills mansion. As a very high-profile business man, Mr Morgan seemed to disapprove of the relationship between Togo and his daughter Nancy. One evening after Nancy arrived home from work, he decided to have a talk with her. I guess he wanted to find out more about Togo and where he was from.

It was late Friday afternoon, and Mr Morgan was having an early evening rest on the third floor of his mansion. Nancy arrived and drove through the main gate in her red and black Mercedes jeep. Suddenly, Mr. Morgan shouted, "Hello Nancy, my dear, I have some very good news for you. Would you like to pop up here for a few minutes?"

Immediately, Nancy exited her jeep and rushed through the large glass doors of the mansion then jumped into the elevator. Shortly after, she arrived on the third floor of the mansion and there was Mr Morgan, looking very disappointed with her. Usually, he would greet his lovely daughter with a peck on her left cheek, but today that wasn't so. As she took a seat by the large glass table, her father reached over and poured her a small glass of ruby-red wine and himself a large Martell brandy. After a few minutes, Mr

Morgan began to speak by saying, "Nancy, my darling, I have noticed that you have found a new friend."

"What friend?" Nancy answered curiously.

"Your boyfriend," Mr Morgan replied. "I also noticed that he has a job working as a caretaker by the old shipyard."

Suddenly Nancy interrupted her father. "Dad, you told me that when I was twenty-one I could have whatever I wanted, like a car, a job or even a boyfriend. Now Dad, what is your problem?"

For a moment, Mr Morgan fell silent, unable to reply to Nancy's question. Then he pulled his long legs from beneath the dining table, rose stood to his feet and walked over to the wine cabinet with caution. He had already finished his Martell brandy, so he decided to celebrate his daughter's special moment with a bottle of pink champagne. He popped it open with pride, then reached over and poured Nancy some in her glass and did the same for himself. They both looked into each other's eyes with love and friendliness, then Mr Morgan replied, "Cheers to you, my daughter, I'm just congratulating you on your accomplishments. I can see that you have a good job and have bought yourself a new car, and now you have found yourself a boyfriend. Now I'm not saying that the boy from the country is the right one, but that is the one you chose. I hope you understand my concern."

A moment later the downstairs phone rang; it was Togo calling from the old shipyard. Immediately, Nancy hurried down the stairs and grabbed hold of the phone as she hit the ground, shouting, "Hello, my sweet."

Togo replied, "Hello my dear, how are you today?"

"I am fine," she replied. "I was just speaking to my father about you and he seems to like you very much, but he's not sure about the job that you are doing as caretaker."

"Hahahaha," Togo laughed. "Don't worry, my dear, I have already applied for a good job in the army, so soon things will be better. I assure you that we will have enough money to spend, and soon we will make it big in this Kingston city. Anyway, I have bought two tickets to go to the cinema."

Before Togo could finish speaking, Nancy dropped the phone and jumped into her jeep to head down to the old shipyard. She collected Togo, and together they spent the evening at the cinema, a sign of true love.

As time went by, together they fell deeper and deeper in love. Usually, Nancy would meet Togo by the bungalow every friday after work. But one very special evening, Togo twenty-first birthday, Nancy decided to spend the day with him, and for the first time Mr Robinson had decided to give Togo a surprise. He drove through the back gate of the old shipyard, slipped out of his car then walked slowly towards the bungalow. He stepped inside the hallway, and there was Nancy Morgan sitting on the couch, looking very beautiful, as Mr Robinson called, "Surprise surprise!" Then Togo rushed from the bedroom and came face to face with his boss, thinking what he was going to say about his girlfriend.

Mr. Robinson greeted him, "Good evening, and how are you?"

"We are all fine, sir," Togo replied.

"I can see that your birthday celebration has already begun. But who is this young lady, may I ask?"

"She is my friend," said Togo.

"And what is your name, young lady?"

"Nancy, Nancy Morgan."

"I guess I've heard that name before. Is your father's name Derek Morgan?"

"Yes sir, you got it just right," she answered.

Mr Robinson already knew a lot about Derek Morgan, including that he owned a multimillion dollar real-estate business on Red Hills Road, so he was very surprised to see his daughter with Togo. For a moment, he thought, then he said, "Nancy, are you a guest or a friend of Togo?"

"No sir, I am not a guest, I am Togo's girlfriend."

Again Mr Robinson was blown away with surprise. Suddenly he turned to Togo with a big smile, saying, "Boy, it seems like tonight you are in for a big birthday treat, so I must go." After giving them his blessing, he then kissed Nancy, shook Togo's hand and left the apartment.

After that it was decision time for Togo and Nancy. They had come to the conclusion that they would like to move in and live together, but there was a problem. Mr Morgan, Nancy's dad, still did not approve of Togo's caretaking job, and Mr Robinson did not give Togo permission to move Nancy into the bungalow. But he also knew that Togo was a very trustworthy young man, and after working with him for over two years Mr Robinson was delighted about Togo's prospects, so he decided to move them away from the bungalow to his private villa across from Hellsha beach. Hellsha is one of the finest areas in Kingston, with fine restaurants, vibrant night clubs and, last but not least, you could see six miles of silver-white sandy beach stretching across the coast. It was an ideal place for a young man to begin his new life.

So late next evening, Mr Robinson decided to visit Togo and surprise him again. It had been a very busy day by the yard. Just as the final visitor was about to check out, in came Mr Robinson with a suspicious look on his face. He greeted Togo saying, "Good evening, son, and how are you?"

"I am fine," Togo replied.

"I know you are fine," Mr Robinson answered, "because after last night with your beautiful girlfriend, it seems to me now that you are enjoying yourself a lot these days."

Togo then turned around, and looked at Mr Robinson with a man-sized smile on his face. He did not even say a word. Then Mr. Robinson looked straight into his eyes, saying, "I noticed that Nancy has been frequently staying by the bungalow, and I will not approve such a thing. However, I know the Morgan family very well and it is true to say that they are multimillionaires, so I am delighted to see you and Nancy together. Here is the key for my private villa. You will occupy the second floor apartment, which has two bedrooms and a lovely bathroom suite, a kitchen and a huge dining room. It even has a wonderful pool outside. At the end of the month, I will withdraw some money from your salary just to cover the bills. So tell me, what you have to say about that?"

For a moment Togo was lost for words, then suddenly he burst out laughing. "Boss I knew you would help me! Trust me, boss, I will never disappoint you, and I know that Nancy will be very happy to hear this. Thank you sir, thank you very much." And with those kind words, the two men shook each other's hands and Mr Robinson left the yard.

So Nancy went to live with Togo. Mr Robinson also promoted him from caretaker to be the managing director of the old shipyard. Nancy still worked as a bartender and a belly dancer. They were very happy living together. A few months later, they decided to get married and start a family, but before long, Nancy had conceived. She gave birth to a stunning baby boy, named Miguel Armstrong. Mr Morgan, Nancy's dad, was delighted of his new grandson, so he gave Nancy and Togo his full support.

Togo writes:

Dear Gal-Gal,

It is now two years since the death of mamma and I have not seen nor heard from you, I sometimes receive letters from Moonhead and Punchinella. They say that they all are doing fine. I am also doing fine, I now have a good job working with Mr Robinson and my girlfriend has now given birth to a stunning baby boy. I wish mamma could see me now. She always told me when I was a child that I was very special and one day I would make it big in the world. Now I can understand what mamma was saying. Gal-Gal, I hope you are fine and may God bless you and keep you, and I wish to hear from you soon. Goodbye.

From brother Togo

Two years later, Nancy gave birth to another stunning baby boy. His name was Adolphus Jr. He also was a blessing to their new family, and they were thinking again about getting married, but Togo had a different idea.

CHAPTER 6
BOARD A SHIP TO AMERICA

As a young man, Togo began to feel a sense of independence; he was thinking before he got married, he wanted to earn enough money to buy a house for his family. "Mr Robinson is a very kind man, and I wish to hand back his key for his private apartment," he thought.

Togo, as the managing director of old shipyard, had access to a lot of very important information about sailings, and he decided to stow away late one night on a ship to America. After a few days of rough sailing, Togo finally reached America, so he decided to head to New York City: New York, New York, the Big Apple, the place where dreams come true. Having left Nancy and his two sons behind, he was very concerned about them, already thinking, "How could I help them?"

The city of New York is a very busy place, so there was not much time to waste. Having a little money, and with quick thinking, you could always find an apartment to rent in Harlem, and that was Togo's first priority. Harlem was not one of the best places to live because of the gang culture; nevertheless, it has a very rich musical heritage. The Apollo recording studio was where some of the greatest American soul artists began, singers like Stevie Wonder, Smokey Robinson, Gladys knight, Marvin Gaye and many more. It was Friday night in New York, and the stars were out to play. As usual, Togo was on his way to the Apollo Broadway Theatre. Just as he arrived at the theatre car park, there approached a red Range Rover Wrangler Jeep with a name license plate on the back. After a moment two men alighted from the vehicle, walking slowly towards the main entrance of the Apollo. Suddenly, one of the men shouted, "Hello man, do I know you from somewhere?"

At the sound of the voice, Togo immediately turned around, and as he gazed across to the far side of the entrance, there was his best friend, Lincoln Bunbun, whom he used to play marbles with after school. After fifteen years, the two men were delighted to see each other again, so they shook hands and began to have a long talk. Along with Bunbun, there was a strange-looking man named Johnny de Silva, a half Jamaican, half Italian, who was a notorious gang leader. Togo was quickly introduced to him, so at once, the three men rolled out together as they left the theatre.

These men were no Johnny-Come-Latelies, and their faces were well known in town. As they drive through Harlem they stopped many times, introducing Togo as their new friend. He became a member of the gang, along with Bunbun, de Silva and One-eyed Barnabas and Jigsaw, two great street fighters, and began thinking about how to make money. Street fighting still remained a very big business in America; that was where Mike Tyson first began. Because Togo had been trained as a cadet, he was no stranger to the rough life, and it was now or never.

Every Saturday night, Harlem was the place to be. Johnny de Silva and his men promoted some of the biggest street fights Harlem had ever seen. From each fight, they made profits of over $20,000 a night. As a member of the gang, Togo was now doing very well. He made sure Nancy and the boys had enough to spend, even though money-laundering is a very serious crime in America, and street fighting was a very dangerous sport.

After a number of years, the gang had made so much money they all bought a lot of property overseas. Togo was now living the American dream, and as a result of his progress, was embarked on a different way of life. From the dark ghetto of Harlem, he now moved to live in the suburbs of New York – a great achievement for an African American even then, and thanks to Martin Luther King, because he was the one who determined that all African Americans should have the right to own houses anywhere in America. America is now a different place from the 1950s and 1960s. Segregation and racism still linger, but are not as prevalent as they used to be in those days.

Togo writes:

Dear Moonhead,

Hello, how are you? Please give my regard to your lovely wife and kids. Things have now changed and I am doing fine. Happy to say I have now bought a new house in the suburbs of New York. I remembered that your dream was to own and run a big electrical business, now is the time I could send some money to help you. So take care and may God bless you.

From Togo

CHAPTER 7
LIFE ON THE EDGE

The gang culture had now become an epidemic in New York, so the government decided that it must come to an end. First, they decided that all gang members must be placed on a list; secondly, all gang members were carefully watched by an FBI surveillance team. Johnny de Silva and his men were no different: they were all wanted by the state. Togo now began to plan his way out. He began to buy a number of shares in the Miami Shipping Association, thinking that one day he would be the owner of one of the biggest shipping companies in America.

Johnny de Silva was now recognised as a multi-millionaire. With his half-Italian background, he had obtained a boxing licence to hold fights in Las Vegas. Jigsaw and Barnabas were no longer street fighters; they too had obtained boxing licences to fight in Las Vegas.

One Friday night, the Las Vegas Theatre had already filled its maximum capacity of 60,000 boxing fans: Johnny de Silva was about to showcase one of the most prestigious fights the year. Appearing from the right corner of the ring, wearing a red-and-blue suit, was Jigsaw the Iron Man. Coming from the left corner, wearing a green-and-white suit, was One-eyed Barnabas, the Leopard Man. All the Americans were on the edges of their seats, waiting to see one of the biggest fights of all time. Standing at ringside were Togo and his best friend Bunbun.

The fight began. In came the Iron Man, face to face with Leopard Man. At once the bell rang and suddenly, they both began to throw punches. Bang, the Leopard Man went down. The referee began to count; in no time, he counted to ten and the fight was over. That was one of the biggest-

money stings the gang ever pulled off. That night, Johnny de Silva and his men walked away with more than $3.5million. (Don't forget they were all from the same gang.)

But the FBI surveillance team now had enough evidence for a conviction, so immediately, their file was turned over to the CIA. The gang had no knowledge that they were under investigation. That Saturday night, the gang leader Johnny de Silva held a liverish party at his Beverly Hills mansion, which as usual was attended by top celebrities and famous movie stars. Togo, as a full member of the gang, was also now enjoying fame and fortune.

Togo writes:

Dear Nancy,
My love, how are you? I have recently received your letter and I
can see that you and the boys are doing fine. I am very busy but I am
doing fine also. I have now achieved enough money to buy a house
for you and the boys. I now believe that I have kept my promise, it's
only a matter of time before I will be home. See you soon

From Togo

Two months later, Johnny de Silva, the famous boxing promoter and notorious gang leader, was brought down in a sting operation by the FBI. He and his men were sentenced to a number of years in a high-security prison in New York. They were all named and shamed by the American government: Togo Armstrong, Lincoln Bunbun, Jigsaw the Iron Man, One-eyed Barnabas the Leopard Man, along with Johnny de Silva himself. They were all charged with money-laundering, their multi-million dollar assets all frozen and under investigation. But as Togo was the son-in-law of Derek Morgan, his multi-million-dollar estate still remained under the Morgan Empire. Togo was now doing time in prison, but Nancy and the boys still enjoyed their new home on Red Hills Road. The US government were still trying to confiscate his estate, but would soon find out how wealthy and powerful Derek Morgan was.

Two years later, the Morgan family decided to get Togo out of prison. So while Nancy was in New York on a visit to see Togo, she decided that she

would pop by to have a word with Sambooka. Daniel Sambooka, one of the highest paid lawyers in New York, never rested a case until the victim was totally free. But first, he would need a good statement from Togo himself, so that the case could be recalled.

Because of Togo, Nancy and the boys were frequently in New York, and in a few weeks Sambooka received the statement. Immediately, he sent an urgent letter to the court, addressed to the magistrate by whom Togo had been tried.

Sambooka writes:

Dear Magistrate,

My name is Daniel Sambooka. I am addressing you as a lawyer under the highest protection of the United States government regarding the case of Togo Armstrong. I have noticed in his case there was not enough evidence regarding his conviction, and so I believe that Mr Armstrong was unlawfully convicted of money-laundering. So in the highest regard of this court, I must please suggest that there be a retrial of the case in regard to Mr Armstrong.

Yours truly,

Daniel Sambooka

A few weeks later Togo was back in court for the second trial. Taking the stand, Mr Sambooka argued, "Your Honour, I see that Mr Armstrong has never been convicted for a crime in the United States, or anywhere in the world, before. So what that tells me, I think, is that Mr Armstrong is a first-time offender. Also the police did not find any substantial amount of money in Mr Armstrong's possession. This is all based on investigation, so I hope you understand the point where I am coming from. I believe that Mr Armstrong should have the right under United States law to an urgent parole appeal."

Six months later, Togo was granted parole and deported back to Jamaica. Once again Togo was enjoying freedom – a lucky man.

CHAPTER 8
GOING TO ENGLAND

During the 1950s and 1960s, England was known as a great superpower. Britain was seen as the melting pot of the developing world. The people from the West Indies, which was still known as the Caribbean, dreamed of getting to England for various reasons. Some went for a better life, some to study or even to help their families. So they would travel by ship or by plane or by any means necessary. They believed that by going to England all their needs would be met and their dreams would be fulfilled.

Aunty Rachel, a fine dressmaker, worked hard all her life trying to earn enough money so that her one and only daughter Dorothy could get to England. The same thing happened with Uncle Balvin. He was a very good fisherman caring for his wife and six children when suddenly one day they decided that they would send Marvin, the oldest son, to England to study. Life was very hard in those days, so even though Uncle Balvin would catch and sell large amount of fish, still he could not earn enough money to buy a plane ticket for his son. He therefore ended up having to sell his one and only fishing boat.

As a young boy growing up in Jamaica, Togo heard lots of story about England, and now he too was planning to go there. So he thought in his mind, "When I was living in America I learnt my lesson, but once I get to England I will be a blessing," and decided to write a letter to his Uncle Troy in England.

Togo writes:

Dear Uncle Troy

How are you? It's about fifteen to twenty years since anyone heard from you. Mama and your sister have already passed away and I have noticed that you did not even bother to attend the funeral.

Anyway, don't worry yourself, Sir. Things are not that great but we are surviving by the grace of God. I have now received a British visa, so soon I will be coming to England. On my arrival I was hoping that you could assist me with a bit of accommodation.

Please give my love to your wife Margaret and your two beautiful daughters Yesmin and Jasmin. Have a good day and I hope to hear from you soon. Thank you sir.

Yours Truly

Togo

The month of January proved to be one of the coldest months in England. Because of the severity of the weather, the temperature remained at 3 degrees centigrade. I guess it was a lovely white Christmas, but all that remained to be seen was a thick layer of black ice which stretched across the city.

It was 8.00am as Togo approached Heathrow Airport. It is still a bit dark, but you could hear the thundering sound of the British Airways plane as it touched down slowly on the runway. Togo alighted from the plane and walked slowly towards the Immigration Department, looking fairly cool and confident. Maybe because of his past experience in America, Togo was not afraid of passing through a large airport.

Uncle Troy and his lovely wife Margaret were already waiting outside in the arrivals lounge. It was about twenty years ago since they had met, so Uncle Troy was hoping that they would recognise each other at first sight, while Togo was thinking the same. The Armstrong family all looked alike. They were tall and sturdy, having a brownish dark complexion, fairly handsome looking, with a bright smile on their faces, so they were easily recognised.

As soon as Togo walked through Immigration, the two men spotted each other. Togo was very happy to see his Uncle Troy, so he ran and hugged him with delight. As they embarked on their long journey home, Togo and his Uncle Troy had a long talk while heading towards Brixton, where his uncle lived. Brixton is one of the busiest areas in London, with lovely restaurants, huge shopping centres and great night clubs for entertainment. People from all nations are found in Brixton, and so it is seen as a multicultural society. It has a large indoor market which is second to none, where you could find everything you wished to buy. The population of Brixton was comprised mainly of West Indians' descendants. In the late 1950s and 1960s, England was experiencing a shortage of manual labour, and so the West Indian community were invited to fill the capacity. They were given jobs like bus drivers, train drivers, nurses and trained engineers to continue the building of the British Railways and other government organisations, and Brixton was where most of these people settled to begin their early hard-working life. Uncle Troy was one of those men, but nowadays he was fully involved in the building trade and worked as a qualified demolition man.

Togo had no trade qualification at all, but with his tough training as a cadet officer in the past, and having spent a little time in a high-security prison in America, he believed that he could adapt to any circumstances. For this reason, his Uncle Troy gave him a few days a week work as a demolition man.

Uncle Troy was a very respected builder, and early in the morning he would gather his men, along with Togo, as they travelled to the outskirts of London, where they would work from 9.00 in the morning until 5.00 in the evening. In London demolition work could be very difficult sometimes, but Togo was determined he would not make the same mistakes he made in the past in America. But after a few months, Togo decided that he did not want to spend all his time working as a demolition man, and so he decided to have a word with his uncle.

It was dinner time, and Margaret was already home from work and was getting ready to serve dinner. Uncle Troy and Togo had just walked through the door after a hard day's work. So they ate dinner, and Margaret then served a bit of rum punch and a slice of carrot cake for afters. They all sat round the table and had a long talk and a good laugh.

"Uncle Troy," Togo muttered, and then carried on, "I am concerned about young people's gang culture. Over the years I have seen a lot of knife crime along with police stop and search. I have seen many youths are going to prison without adequate evidence, and it goes on and on. I know that having a trade in England is good, but I would like to go back to college and do a course, and work as a youth worker. I know with my past experience it would be beneficial to many of these young people. So I would like to work three days a week and go to college for two days."

Uncle Troy was a God-fearing man, and was delighted for Togo to achieve what was his heart's desire. So as a family they all agreed, and in a few months Togo enrolled in a college and started attending. He also decided to change his job from a demolition man to work as a main-shift security guard.

CHAPTER 9
LIVING IN LONDON

After a year, Togo was doing well in London. He now had a good part-time job, and was due to graduate next summer as a fully trained youth leader. London is a very lovely place to be in summer, so Togo decided to enjoy its culture. The Queen's Diamond Jubilee was a one-off celebration, and very extravagant. More than a thousand boats floated along the Thames,

while Navy and Army men dressed in ceremonial costumes participated in the big celebrations. The wedding of Prince Charles and Princess Diana still remains one of the greatest events that ever happened in London, televised and watched by more than two million people around the world. The Princess was noted as a champion of charity organisations, and her charitable work touched the lives of some of the poorest nations around the world. In Africa and Asia, the reach of her kind and loving generosity is still evident. Until this day her untimely death is still seen as a mystery in the eyes of many people, and I believe that the half has never yet been told. Princess Diana has now become a legend and her work still continues – she is still recognised as an influential human being.

London has also seen the wedding of Prince William and Princess Kate which was carefully watched by over two million people. They are now seen as the modern-day champions of charity, but their lives are still unfolding as the people carefully watch and wait to see their progress.

The beautiful game of football occurs every Saturday evening, where a lot of people from different background gather together to watch the game. Togo and his friends would come together at their local pub and sit with a drink and snack to watch the match of the day. As a footballer in London, you could earn over one hundred thousand pounds per week. It is true to say that David Beckham has now become an ambassador for England. His career started from playing football. And the city of London is about to host one of the greatest games in the world, the Olympic Games. Togo was thinking, "Now I have got a good chance to see London in all its glory. It is a time of celebration, a time when the nations of the world are coming

to London to perform some their greatest sportsmanship of all time. London is one of the most beautiful cities I have ever lived in. I can now see my life changing dramatically, and in a few years from now I will be recognised as one of the greatest youth leaders in London, but for the moment I will enjoy myself to best of my ability."

Jamaica is one of the island in the West Indies which has been producing some of the greatest track and field runners of all time, one of whom is Usain Bolt. Over the years thousands of visitors have come to London to enjoy the city, and the big red bus has played a very vital part in their transportation. However, London has also experienced some very dark moments in its history, like the constant bombing of the IRA. Also, on 7 July 2008 London saw a very dangerous terrorist attack on its transportation network system which claimed the lives of many people. They also experienced the great Tottenham riot of 2011, which spread across London like wildfire. However, the people of London responded with great courage and strength by determining in themselves that nothing will dampen their spirits. Hence more power to the people of London, the greatest city on earth.

CHAPTER 10
TOGO FOUND STRENGTH

Two years later, Togo graduated from college as a qualified youth leader and had a chance to seek employment as a social worker. However, because of his past record in America, he had to undergo the Criminal Record Bureau (CRB) checks which are now a requirement in England. The British government recommend that everyone who works as a youth leader or social worker or even in the medical field must have a CRB check certificate. Luckily Togo did not have a criminal record in England, and he was offered a job as a social worker.

Living in London for a number of years, Togo has now seen the struggle and peer pressure that faces young people. As a youth leader, he recognised how challenging it could be working with youths, and he decided to start an organisation for young people known as Street Talk. It is an organisation which accommodates young people from all over London. At the end of each month, Togo arranges to meet more than 250 young people who come together from different parts of London. Each person that attends the meeting is there to find out more about issues affecting their lives. Also some are there to discuss issues that they have seen happening in and around their community, for example the stop and search exercise carried out by the police. Other issues are graduating from college or university and not being able to obtain employment; and the unpleasant name "yob" which is used to stigmatise young people because of anti-social behaviour. It is known that stigmatising young people can result in a negative attitude towards their development.

Therefore Togo was determined that the name "yob" should be changed to "Brod". The word Brod means brothers and sisters coming and working together as one. Togo decided that for the young people to see any kind of change, he would have to invite the Mayor of London to attend some of the monthly meetings, therefore he decided to send the Mayor an urgent letter through the post.

Letter to the Mayor of London from Togo:

Dear Sir,

My name is Togo Armstrong and I have been working as a social worker for a number of years and have now become a community youth leader.

In respect of the youths in the community, we have now developed a youth organisation known as Street Talk. We have enrolled more than three thousand and five hundred young people as members of Street Talk. At the end of every month, all the youths come together from different parts of London to discuss issues affecting their lives in their communities.

In respect of your highly regarded status and position, we would like to invite you to sit on one of the panels of one of our monthly meetings. We are pleased to inform you that we are dearly looking forward to your commitment to fulfil our request.

Thanking you for your cooperation.
Yours faithfully
Togo Armstrong

A few weeks later, Togo received a reply letter from the Mayor, indicating that he is more than happy to do so. He also mentioned in the letter that whatever assistance the organisation needed, he would be happy to help meet them. He mentioned that as from now, a substantial amount of funding will be also available for the development of the community, especially in the areas of music, art, writing and sport. Now Togo was on the move to transform the communities with his experience from the past. Likewise, Street Talk youth organisation has become one of the best-recognised youth group in London. They are the ones who are now trying to bring about changes towards knife crime and gun violence. Both young and old in the community have strongly supported Togo's ideas. With the help of the Mayor, he has now launched another charity known as Helping Hand.

Helping Hand is an organisation which assists older people in the community. Over two hundred young people are now volunteering to assist the older people on a daily basis. Every day we hear on the news that older people are suffering in their homes because of having no one to visit them or help them. Togo and the other youths have now volunteered to give a helping hand, such as with their weekly shopping and collecting their medication from the pharmacy. They are also making sure that if they are having problems with their utility bills like gas, water or electricity, they can inform the council.

It is so true to say that no man is an island, but if a group of people coming together by supporting each other they could make a difference to the lives of many. However, the Mayor has now seen the positive impact that a youth organisation can have on young people, and decided that the British Government must be informed about the organisation Street Talk.

As the founder and leader of Street Talk, Togo decided to organise one of the biggest youth festivals, which is to be held in the Hyde Park. For this event the Prime Minister and his Deputy will be guests of honour. Over twenty thousand young people are expected to attend this festival, which will feature a number of cultural activities like sports, music, dancing, book reading and many more.

On the occasion, the Prime Minister will give a speech about the development and positive changes that the young people are contributing to the society. He will also be paying tribute to people like David Beckham, Usain Bolt and Togo Armstrong, who are now seen as the modern role models.

Togo was very happy to receive such a great honour from the British Government. What we are seeing here is how other young people could use their talents to the best of their ability to bring changes to the lives of others.

One good thing we have learned in this book is how we can begin to make changes to our communities. We have also learned how the life of a human being can be transformed, from the depths of despair into the pinnacle of success. I know we can succeed if we all begin to make positive changes in our own lives, then use these ideas to transform the world.

Togo has now enjoyed a greater level of success because of his commitment to changing himself for the better, and this dedication and commitment has now been turned towards changing the community for the better. Togo believes that life is what you make it, and if you will only look within yourself, then we all can make this world a better place to live.

CHAPTER 11
THE GIFT OF LIFE

In the beginning God created the heavens and the earth. As we have all read in the book of Genesis, chapter 1, God gave men life and abundance. We all know that mankind was not born to suffer from diseases and sickness, but because mankind has made themselves slaves to sin, the desolation of diseases and sickness have come upon them. However, if people will live according to the commandments of God as stated in the Bible, then they will be free from all these diseases and sickness.

Unfortunately Togo was no different. At the tender age of twenty-five, he was facing the same disease that for twenty-five years dominated the life of his father Mr Armstrong. It was kidney disease, which could be a very dangerous sickness, but thanks be to God for the achievements in the medical field, Togo has now got a chance to receive first-class medical treatment from the National Health Service (NHS) in England. He could even receive a kidney transplant from the NHS. Also, by changing his diet and doing lots of exercise, Togo has now been able to recover and overcome the disease. Thanks to the hard-working doctors and nurses who made it possible for Togo to be alive today.

I am Togo Armstrong. Thanks be to God that I am now fit and well, as my family and I are enjoying the gift of a new life. This story is a true story, and I believe it will remain in the back of our minds until the end of time.